34 delicio
recipes

Displaced
Dishes

that found their
way to Samos
Refugee Camp

S

Preface to the third edition

This book was first published in December 2018. The goal was to raise funds for the NGO Samos Volunteers and support the free services they offer to people going through the asylum process on Samos island.

Since then, we've sold thousands of copies, reprinted the book in German, and donated around € 60,000 to Samos Volunteers.

The situation on Samos continues to evolve and this third print run of the English version of Displaced Dishes reflects that fact. The newly-added Winter 2022 update provides an overview of the current situation; including information on the new camp, an interview with a resident and a report on how Samos Volunteers has adapted.

This edition also contains a brand new recipe for a wonderful Malian stew, Tigadegena (see page 86).

Thank you so much for buying the book and supporting the vital work of Samos Volunteers.

Author, recipe collection and co-editor
Pamela Gregory

Co-author, photography and co-editor
Gregory Oke

Co-editor, project coordination
Natalia Karacaoglu

Design and layout
Konstantin Zhukov

A special thank you to Lindsay Maitland-Hunt for
her help and assistance with the recipe editing.

First published by Gregory Oke, December 2018.
2nd edition printed November 2019.
3nd edition printed November 2022.

Contact info@displaceddishes.com
for orders and inquiries.

displaceddishes.com

Printed in Lithuania by KOPA.

ISBN: 978-1-5272-3212-9

Contents

Displaced Dishes

Displaced Dishes started when Pam Gregory decided to work with Samos Volunteers (SV), an organisation that provides services to people living in the makeshift refugee camp on the Greek island of Samos. With a background in the restaurant business and culinary world, Pam found herself connecting with the residents through the subject of food. She decided to start collecting people's favourite recipes from back home with the aim of producing a fundraising cookbook. With Pam's ongoing work and the combined efforts of Gregory Oke, Natalia Karacaoglu and Konstantin Zhukov, that aim has been realised. We're proud to present Displaced Dishes.

With 34 recipes from 12 different countries, this book is a real culinary treat for the reader. Each delectable dish is accompanied by succinct personal memories and tips from the recipe contributors themselves. From sumptuous salads and flavoursome vegetarian feasts to mouthwatering meat dishes and irresistible desserts, this small book offers something for everybody!

However, the aim of the book extends beyond just providing the reader with exciting and authentic food ideas. It is also a snapshot of the complexity and ongoing tragedy of the European refugee crisis. On the macro level, the wide array of countries from which our contributors were forced to leave, and the sheer distance they travelled to reach Samos, demonstrates the scale of modern displacement. Whilst on the human level, these donated recipes provide an insight into the very personal loss displacement brings.

Painful separation from one's culture, homeland and family, are all tied up with the celebration of food from home. We're extremely grateful to the contributors for sharing these meaningful recipes.

Everyone involved in this project, through the phases of recipe collection, editing, testing, photographing, and finally design, donated their time and services entirely for free. The book is therefore a testament to our collective desire to improve the living conditions of people attempting to seek refuge in Europe. We've made huge efforts with the descriptions and layouts of the recipes so that we can feel confident that this book is worth every penny of the asking price on its merits as a cookbook alone. However, we also feel extremely proud that 100% of the money made from the sale of this book will go directly to Samos Volunteers. This is an organisation that many of us have worked for and that we know from first-hand experience provides vital support to the refugee population from which these recipes originally came.

Thank you for choosing to purchase Displaced Dishes. We hope the recipes enclosed bring you and your loved ones a great deal of joy.

Recipe Collector, Pam

It doesn't matter which country you're from or which religion you follow, the thing that unites all of us is our love of good food and the opportunity to sit down and relax with friends and family to enjoy a leisurely meal, lovingly prepared and appreciatively eaten. It is one of the greatest pleasures in life and one of the things that displaced people miss most.

Working with the organisation Samos Volunteers (SV) provided plenty of opportunities to talk to people about their lives and experiences and it was a genuine revelation to discover how many fond memories involved getting together and sharing food. Conversations about their homeland and culture invariably turned into long, nostalgic descriptions of the much cherished home cooking they regularly enjoyed as a family, or the special Once A Year meal that would be organised for a Feast Day. Women missed the opportunity to express their love and care for their families by cooking delicious meals on a daily basis. Teenagers would compete loudly with one another to describe their family's particular way of making pilau and elderly eyes would mist over recalling the whole day that their grandmother spent making the perfect Lahmajoun, only to see it enthusiastically demolished in seconds by ravenous diners!

SV holds regular dinners at their Alpha Centre in Samos town where unaccompanied minors (refugees under 18 years old travelling without their families) are invited to sit down to a homecooked meal created and served by both refugees and volunteers like myself. The meals

Gregory's foreword

are usually followed by enthusiastic dancing to fantastic music from back home. These evenings create further opportunities for the guests to chat about foods they miss most. It was from these conversations that the idea of Displaced Dishes was born. I began to write down and collect people's favourite recipes.

The result is a colourful and varied collection of dishes gathered from lots of keen contributors, representing many different countries and cultures. Each contributor was more than happy to give their time and expertise to the project, and they were united in their desire to see the book published and their names in print! This is the perfect present for anyone who loves making wonderful, slightly out of the ordinary food.

Bil-hana-wa ash shifa – may you enjoy your meal with gladness and health!

From port to camp to

Samos Volunteers (SV) is a grassroots movement of volunteers from around the world who came together in autumn 2015 to respond to the escalating refugee crisis. Samos island's location, only a few kilometres from the Turkish coast, meant that it received huge numbers of refugees in the summer of 2015, many fleeing the war in Syria. The UNHCR and Greek authorities established a makeshift facility at Malagari port to shelter the new arrivals. The crisis was in its infancy and SV's role was in the provision of basic needs: food, water and blankets.

In March 2016, everything changed once the much-contested EU-Turkey Deal was introduced and implemented, resulting in an even greater influx of refugees and longer stays on the island. People were gradually transferred from the port to a former army barracks that had been converted to what authorities refer to as a Reception and Identification Centre (RIC) or a 'Hotspot'. However, its residents and SV simply called this place 'Camp'.

What had begun as a group of individuals supporting local residents and providing emergency assistance was organically developing into the established team of short-term, long-term, and community volunteers that it is today. With the establishment of the original Camp, SV continued to meet the new arrival's basic needs by distributing tents, blankets, clothes, shoes, and hygiene products. In addition to that, SV started to alleviate pressure on the NGOs present on the island by offering informal language classes and activities to the most vulnerable families.

Images of the original Camp on Samos in 2019

Displaced

entre and beyond

In Spring 2017, SV shifted focus from its distribution program to psychosocial activities by expanding its language classes to cater to various learner types and starting fun activities for children, teens and adults. The group quickly realised they needed somewhere to house their resources, classes, and the ever expanding number of beneficiaries who accessed the services. As a result, in July of the same year, SV opened the doors to the island's only refugee community centre – the much-adored Alpha Centre.

The Alpha is a three storey building with six multi use classroom/activity spaces, a nursery section and two large communal areas. It is open seven days a week, staffed solely by SV volunteers, totally free and a short walk from the site of the original Vathy Camp.

2018 saw the Alpha Centre go from strength to strength and it's usage grow. SV continued to adapt to meet the needs of the camp's population, opening a hugely popular laundry service and a new law clinic.

With the refugee crises falling from the front pages of the news and the departure of other NGOs from the island, SV's work became more important than ever. In late 2019, the population of the original camp was at its highest since 2015. Over 6200 people were housed in facilities designed to accomodate ony 650[1].

Many people were living in makeshift tents and shelters they had built themselves. The danger of such overcrowding was terrifyingly exposed in ▶

October 2019 when a fire tore through a section of the camp. Miraculously there were no fatalities, but around 600 people lost both their dwellings and the belongings that they'd brought with them from their homeland. On the night of the fire, the Alpha Centre was opened immediately as an emergency shelter, with all available space being used to accommodate those in need.

Despite no longer being widely reported upon, the situation on Samos remains a humanitarian crisis. SV and its volunteers continue to work tirelessly to improve the situation for refugees on Samos. Through their classes, activities and services they help instil a sense of normality, combat boredom, and provide a space outside of the camp for socialising and events. However, the charity needs all the support it can get to continue to offer this vital assistance. This is why 100% of profits from this book will be donated directly to Samos Volunteers.

[1] Data from the Hellenic Republic Ministry of Interior National Co-ordination Centre for Border Control Immigration and Asylum.

Images fom @samosvolunteers Instagram account

Winter 2022 update

A new camp

Since 2016, life in the original 'Camp' on Samos was characterised by systematic overcrowding. Centred in, and later sprawling around a facility designed to accommodate 650 people, the camp's population at times exceeded 8,000. Those arriving in Samos to seek asylum were not issued papers for onward travel to mainland Greece and were forced to wait as their cases were processed, sometimes for years.

NGOs and aid agencies consistently called for people waiting on Samos to be transferred away from the deteriorating situation there, yet little action was taken. Authorities continued to gamble with the lives of the camp residents, who faced unsanitary and dangerous living conditions, including persistent outbreaks of fire. In 2020, at the height of the first wave of Covid-19, the camp's population was ten times over capacity with conditions clearly the antithesis of what would be considered safe or responsible during a pandemic. Even then, the authorities continued the policy of containment.

However, in early 2021, the Greek government suddenly accelerated the issuing of documents. In a turbulent six months, around 3,000 people left the island, either by their own means or as part of official transfers organised by Greek asylum authorities. Clearly, the system can work more efficiently when it is deemed convenient by the authorities. Depressingly, it appears the sudden change in policy was motivated not by humanitarian grounds, but political ones. ▶

On the 18th of September 2021, a new 'Closed Controlled Access Centre' (C.C.A.C.) was inaugurated on the island of Samos. The opening event was attended by representatives from national and EU governing bodies. It was the first of a 250 million euro EU-funded project that will see the construction of larger, more isolated and highly controlled camps on the five 'hotspot' islands. With the facilities on Lesvos, Chios, Kos and Leros still under construction (those on Leros and Kos subsequently opened late 2021), Samos became something of a poster child for the new scheme, with the dramatic increase in transfers away from the island, an apparent attempt to present a more orderly picture in time for the new camp's inauguration.

Situated in Zervou, an arid, hilly area in the centre of the island, the new C.C.A.C. has a capacity of around 3,000 people. As of September 2022, there are approximately 900 residents.

Material living conditions have improved, although still basic and clinical. Housing consists of iso-box containers, fitted with beds, cooking stands, refrigeration, and air conditioning. However, these necessities only look like the much publicised 'dignified accommodation' when viewed in comparison to the horrendous conditions of the past half decade. Given the 43 million euros invested in the Samos C.C.A.C. alone, there are remarkable deficiencies in camp amenities and new residents have already reported malfunctioning electrics, leaking containers and unfinished construction.

Most worrying are the disproportionate use of security measures and the camp's new location. The C.C.A.C. is surrounded by a double barbed wire fence, and residents are subject to airport-style security and a night curfew from 8.00 pm to 8.00 am. In contrast to the original camp, which was 5 minutes walk from Vathy Town, the new site is located 7 km away. There is a bus service, but it costs € 3.20 for a return trip, which is prohibitively expensive, considering the average assistance received per person is € 70 per month and residents didn't even receive that between October and December 2021 due to an 'administrative error' on the part of the Greek government.

These constraints have effectively cut residents' access to vital infrastructure and support services which have been built up in Vathy over the last five years. Physical and mental health provisions, as well as integration prospects, appear totally absent from the planned reception strategy. The people subjected to this 'welcome', along with local solidarity groups and NGOs, and even the EU's very own Fundamental Rights Agency have all expressed deep concerns about such confined isolation and the impact it will have on mental health.

The strategy seems clear: to completely isolate the refugee population in panopticon-style, high security facilities. To remove asylum seekers from local and international sight and when they are visible, to outwardly portray them as illegal migrants or as criminals, by housing them in facilities that not only resemble, but function like prisons.

Seeking asylum is not a crime. It is an entirely legal and comprehensible action when the situation in one's home country is unsafe or untenable. The opening of the Samos C.C.A.C. exemplifies the disturbing direction of the EU's already shameful migration and asylum policy.

Life in the new camp

For privacy reasons, we haven't shared our interviewee's name. They also asked that we conduct the interview over an encrypted chat using voice messages to guarantee their anonymity.

Residents feel justifiably cautious about speaking out or sharing information about the C.C.A.C from the inside. There have been reprisals when images and interviews have been traced back to their source by camp officials. These kinds of informal intimidation tactics put further strain on residents' freedom of speech and stifle their right to protest.

What follows is the transcript of the voice messages.

 **Voice note
10.36 am**

Yes, I'm in the new camp now. I think many people are interested to hear about life here. I can say it is like a prison. With barbed wire and fences. You can't go outside if you don't have an ID. If you don't have an ID you don't go to school, you don't go to hospital, you don't go to the town to buy food.

 **Voice note
10.37 am**

When we were transferred to the new camp, not everybody got or had an ID card. Many people arrived without one. Since we got to the new camp, everybody's application for ID cards has been slow or rejected. I have one friend here, he has been rejected four times. They tell him he can't appeal again but must wait. They say 'just wait, just wait'. Here it is very bad.

**Voice note
10.40 am**

Yes, if you don't have an ID they say you can't go outside. Since I arrived two years ago I've always been studying English [through the free courses offered by Samos Volunteers]. Now it is even more helpful because it allows me to leave the new camp, because I have a reason. They [the camp authorities] get the names of the students who are studying with the NGO and they check that we are a student before they let us leave.

**Voice note
10.41 am**

So if we want to leave and we have class at the school, then we can leave. But if we just want to go outside and we don't have class they don't allow us. It's no good. It really is just like a prison.

**Voice note
10.50 am**

Again, we are here and we haven't received any financial assistance for the last four months [the UNHCR used to run the cash assistance ▶

programme, whereby individuals in the asylum process would receive a small sum of, on average, €70 per month. However, this responsibility was transferred to the Greek government in October. Since the transfer of responsibility, the government has failed to provide any financial support to the people who are eligible. It has now been almost four months in which there has been no cash assistance]. **If we don't have any money how can we do anything for ourselves? Even a little.**

**Voice note
10.51 am**

This is breakfast and this is lunch. We didn't get dinner today. Finished.

The food they give us here is no good. When we were in the old camp many people received a little money from UNHCR and then if you don't like the food in the camp you can walk to the supermarket and buy some food to cook for yourself in your tent, you can eat! But since we moved to the new camp we don't have this option. We're left hungry by the food they give us here. It's really not very good food, not healthy and the portions are very small, just like in the old camp – except now it's more difficult to go and buy your own food. You understand?

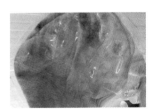

We can't afford good fresh food, like good meat or green vegetables, healthy fresh food that makes you feel good.

Images: breakfast and lunch on the day of the interview.

Voice note
10.54 am

If you have a problem and need to see the doctor. For example, last week I went to the camp doctor and he gave me a prescription. He said he doesn't have the medicine I need and I must go to the pharmacy. But the medicine costs me € 14! As a refugee I can't afford this. Since arriving in Samos I've had so many problems like this.

Voice note
10.56 am

I've been here two years on Samos. For me the difference between the new camp and the old camp – actually not just for me, but a lot of people feel the same way – the old camp was better for us. When we were in the old camp, when you needed something you could just walk to the town, easily. If you had one euro or two euros, you can walk fast to the city buy some food and cook, easy. For example, spaghetti or some food that you like from home, you can cook it and make it. They say the conditions here are better, but our containers leak. Whenever it rains, it's leaking.

Image: rain dripping into the container, screenshot of a video.

Voice note
10.57 am

When we moved here to the new camp, if you don't have transport you can't go to the town. So if you have only € 5 or € 10 to spend, the bus to go to the town costs € 1.60 to get to there and € 1.60 to come back. It's too much. We can't afford it. Your money is finished. ▶

Voice note
10.59 am

How are we meant to do anything like this? We are all humans, but for me, we in the camp just feel like items. We are like goods kept in a shop.

Voice note
11.00 am

We don't have anything to do. If you don't study, you just sleep. We can play a bit of football inside the camp. But if you don't like football, you sleep. We don't have any work, we don't have anything to do.

Image: Samos Volunteers newly opened Alpha Land.

Samos Volunteers' re

From July 2021, Samos Volunteers (SV) began renting a small field now dubbed Alpha Land, located 5 minutes walk from the new Zervou camp. Setting up a tented space in close proximity to the new camp was essential to ensure continuity in their provision of services to those confined in the isolated facility.

Alpha Land now allows for a Welcome Area, three classrooms, a women's space and other areas for additional activities such as sewing classes, conversation labs, music sessions, bike maintenance, art workshops and much more.

SV have also managed to continue their ever-popular free laundry service. Through the use of a Laundry Van, SV are now able to reach the new camp every morning, where they receive residents' laundry bags, and bring back their clothes, washed and dried, in the evening.

For the moment, the Alpha Centre in Vathy remains open to provide drop-in services, women-only activities and afternoon language classes, whilst the Alpha Hub has been re-purposed as a space for legal-aid NGOs to meet their clients.

Samos Volunteers will maintain its work on Samos for as long as support and aid are needed. They will also continue to advocate for the abolition of the EU practice of mass confinement and surveillance, and publicly demand sustainable, dignified accommodation and integration solutions for all people seeking asylum in Europe.

onse

Visit the Samos Volunteers
website to find out more
and to donate:
samosvolunteers.org

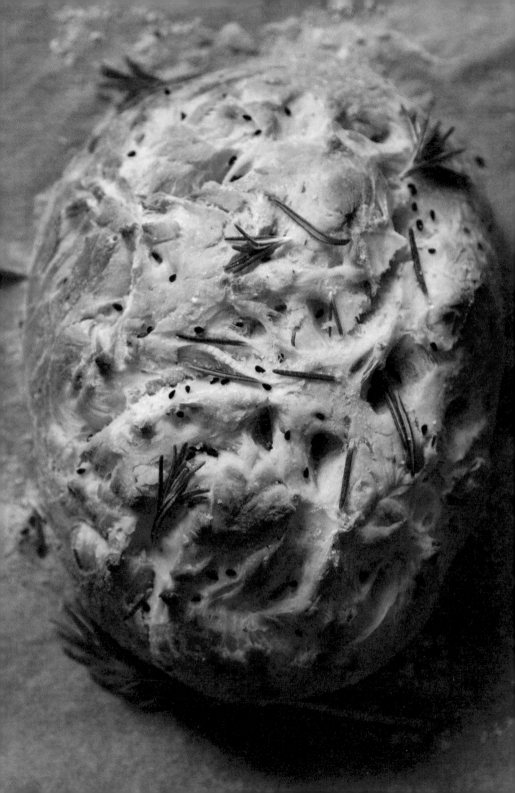

Spiked rosemary bread

Recipe provided by **Hamid** from **Iran**
Makes one loaf

Hamid says this recipe originates from way back when his family lived in Bukhara in Uzbekistan. It's a very aromatic bread and particularly lovely teamed with smoked fish, or topped with goats cheese mixed with a few torn basil leaves.

150 ml warm water
1 tablespoon honey
500 g strong white flour
1 tablespoon instant yeast
1 tablespoon roughly chopped fresh rosemary leaves
2 teaspoons salt
¾ teaspoon ras el hanout
1 large egg, beaten
3 tablespoons sunflower or olive oil, plus a little for brushing
1 tablespoon nigella seeds

In a small bowl, mix the honey and warm water until the honey is dissolved. In a large bowl, stir the flour, yeast, rosemary, salt, and ras el hanout until combined. Pour in the water mixture, beaten egg and oil. Mix carefully and knead together to form a smooth ball of dough. You may need to add a little more water if the mix seems a bit dry.

When the dough is smooth, brush it lightly with oil, cover the bowl with a clean towel, and store in a warm place until the dough has doubled in size, about an hour.

Heat your oven to 200 °C, gas mark 6.

Knead the dough again until all the air has gone and until it is smooth. Place it on a lightly floured baking sheet and shape it into a large, flat oblong shape, about 3 to 4 cm thick. Cover and leave to rise until doubled in size.

When the dough has doubled in size, take a pair of sharp scissors, hold them upright, and snip the dough roughly every inch or so into ▶

sharp peaks. Brush with a little more oil and
sprinkle with the nigella seeds.

Place the sheet in the centre of the oven for
10 minutes, then rotate front to back and reduce
the heat to 180 °C, gas mark 4. Bake for 10 more
minutes, or until nicely browned.

Challah

Recipe provided by **Ayad** from **Palestine**
Makes one loaf

This is a wonderful rich bread from Palestine. Ayad remembers his auntie getting up very early in the morning on special days to make sure it was hot and out of the oven by lunchtime.

250 ml warm water
2 teaspoons caster sugar
450 g strong white flour
7 g dried instant yeast
1 teaspoon salt
2 large eggs, beaten
1 egg yolk, for glazing
1 teaspoon poppy seeds
1 teaspoon sesame seeds

In a large bowl, combine the flour, yeast, and salt. Dissolve the sugar in the warm water in a small bowl and then pour over the flour mixture. Add the eggs, then use your hands to knead everything into a smooth dough. Add a little more flour if the mixture is too sticky.

Knead for 10 minutes more, until the dough is smooth and elastic. Cover the bowl with a clean tea towel and leave in a warm place until the dough has risen to double its size, about 35 minutes.

Preheat your oven to 180 °C, gas mark 4. Punch the dough down and knead again for 3 minutes, then shape into a plain loaf or a three strip plait. Place the loaf on a baking tray and let rise until doubled in size, about 30 minutes more.

Mix the egg yolk with a little water, then brush the loaf. Sprinkle evenly with the poppy and sesame seeds.

Bake until golden brown, about 40 minutes.

Laxoox

Recipe provided by **Djamila** from **Djibouti**
Makes 8, 20cm Laxoox

Laxoox is a flat, spongy bread from Djibouti. Similar to neighbouring Ethiopia's Injera bread, it has a delicious sour taste that comes from the dough's overnight fermentation process. Djamila says they're eaten with almost all meals; at breakfast with banana and honey, or her favourite, with spicy fried tomatoes and eggs. They're also great for tearing and scooping up stews and sauces. (See page 76 for a spicy lentil dish, also from Djibouti). It's very quick and easy to mix up a batch of these for the next morning, and when you taste them you won't regret it!

2 cups plain flour
½ cup rice flour or
  sorghum flour if available
1½ teaspoons salt
1 teaspoon sugar
1½ teaspoons yeast
2½ cups lukewarm water
2 teaspoons vegetable oil
  for cooking

Add all the ingredients for the batter to a large mixing bowl. Whisk until you have a smooth consistency with no lumps. Cover and leave to ferment in the fridge overnight, allowing enough space in the bowl for the mixture to expand by around 20%. If there's no space in the fridge for a big mixing bowl, leaving overnight in a cool dry place works well too. The mixture should look bubbly and frothy by the next morning. Before cooking give it another good stir making sure to mix in any parts that may have separated overnight.

Heat a large non stick pan over medium heat. Add the oil, spreading it evenly across the whole area of the pan with some kitchen roll.

Add a ladle of the mixture to the middle of the pan and allow it to spread out naturally. Cook for 4-5 minutes on a medium heat and do not flip. When it's ready it should be cooked through with the bottom a golden brown colour.

Dukkah

This is a much loved aromatic spice mix containing ground nuts, intended to be sprinkled on dishes just before eating. It's quick and easy to make a jamjar of dukkah to keep on the spice rack. It's not only delicious with soups, fragrant stews and roasted vegetables, but is great on salads too. Use as a rub to marinate meat before cooking, or sprinkle on top of yoghurt to make a tasty dip.

Although this recipe was not given to us directly by a resident of the camp, dukkah does pop up a lot in refugees descriptions of food from the Middle East.

70 g hazelnuts, toasted
3 tablespoons coriander
  seeds
2 tablespoons sunflower
  seeds, toasted
1½ tablespoons sesame
  seeds
1 tablespoon cumin seeds
1 tablespoon dried green
  peppercorns, or black
  peppercorns if you can't
  find green
1 teaspoon fennel seeds
1 teaspoon sweet paprika
1 teaspoon salt
½ teaspoon nigella seeds

Combine all the ingredients in a grinder or a small food processor and pulse until you have a lumpy powder.

Aubergine caviar

Recipe provided by **Mohammed** from **Iraq**
Makes a dip for 4-6

Also known as babaghanoush, this alternative to hummus is eaten throughout the Middle East. Mohammed guarantees it will convert anyone who claims to not like aubergine.

3 medium aubergines, halved lengthwise
3 cloves garlic, minced
2 tablespoons lemon juice, plus more if desired
3 tablespoons tahini
1/3 cup extra virgin olive oil
1/2 cup chopped fresh parsley leaves
raw vegetable sticks or flatbread for serving

Preheat your oven to 200 °C, gas mark 6, with a rack positioned in the centre.

Line a baking sheet with aluminum foil or parchment paper. Place the aubergines cut side down and roast until charred and completely tender, 35 to 40 minutes. Use a spoon to scoop out the roasted flesh into a large bowl. Discard the skins.

Add the garlic and lemon juice to the roasted aubergine and mix thoroughly to make a paste. Stir in the tahini and then the olive oil in a steady stream until the mixture is pale and creamy. Stir in the parsley and season with salt and more lemon juice, if desired.

Serve with raw vegetable sticks or flatbread. It's also wonderful with some big, fat crispy chips sprinkled with sea salt.

Dibs tahini

Recipe provided by **Rania** from **Kuwait**
Makes a starter/dip for 4

Rania from Kuwait who gave us this recipe describes it as a 'Middle Eastern version of peanut butter and jelly'. It looks sumptuous when swirled all together. A very rich dish.

½ cup tahini
¼ cup water
2 garlic cloves, minced
¼ cup pomegranate
   molasses
salt and black pepper

Whisk the tahini and water in a small bowl until smooth. Stir in the garlic, then season to taste with salt and pepper.

To serve, pour the pomegranate molasses into a serving bowl, then cover with the tahini mixture. Serve as is in two layers, or stir together if you'd prefer it mixed.

Muhammara

Recipe provided by **Amran** from **Syria**
Makes a dip for 4-6

This is gorgeous! One of Syria's much-loved national dishes. Muhammara is a thick spicy dip which is vegetarian, unbelievably delicious and full of healthy ingredients. This particular version comes from Amran who hails from northern Syria and inherited the recipe from his beloved Mum who is sadly no longer with him.

5 tablespoons olive oil, divided
1 large onion, finely chopped
2 garlic cloves, chopped
1 packed cup chopped roasted red peppers
1 cup walnuts, toasted
¼ cup breadcrumbs
2 teaspoons pomegranate molasses
1 teaspoon lemon juice
1 teaspoon ground cumin
1 teaspoon chilli flakes
salt and pepper
toast or pita bread for serving

Heat 1 tablespoon of the oil in a large frying pan over medium-high heat. Add the onion, garlic, and 1 teaspoon salt. Cook, stirring often, until the onions are translucent and soft, 10 to 12 minutes. Transfer to the bowl of a food processor and add the remaining ingredients. Pulse until you have a thick, chunky paste. Season to taste with salt and pepper.

Serve with toast or pita bread.

Fattoush

Recipe provided by **Riz** from **Kurdistan**
Makes a side salad for 4

A lovely crunchy salad made with chunks of crispy fried bread. Riz from Kurdistan, who offered the recipe, insists that only pita bread will do, but we discovered that fried cubes of soft, white doughy bread can also give the salad a wonderful texture.

1 tablespoon olive oil, for frying
2 pita breads, torn into pieces, or one Arabic flatbread
2 tablespoons extra virgin olive oil
1 tablespoon lemon juice
1 teaspoon ground sumac, plus more for serving
1 garlic clove, crushed
1 head romaine lettuce, torn or sliced
½ large cucumber, halved and thinly sliced
2 medium tomatoes, sliced, or a handful cherry tomatoes, or a mix of both
½ red onion, thinly sliced
2 tablespoons torn mint leaves
2 tablespoons chopped fresh parsley leaves
sea salt and black pepper

Fry the bread:
Heat the vegetable oil in a straight-sided frying pan over medium-high heat. Add the torn pita and cook, turning gently to fry all sides, until golden brown. Transfer to a paper towel-lined plate and let cool. Alternatively you can toast or grill the pita but Riz recommends frying!

Make the dressing:
Whisk the olive oil, lemon juice, sumac, and garlic together in a large bowl. Season to taste with salt and pepper. Add the romaine, cucumber, tomatoes, red onion, and herbs and toss to combine. Fold in the crisped pita slices, sprinkle generously with sumac and more herbs, if you'd like, and serve.

Watermelon and feta salad

Recipe provided by **Maryam** from **Palestine**
Makes a side salad for 4

This is a delicious fresh salad from Palestine. Maryam says that in the absence of Feta, any sharp-flavoured white crumbly cheese will complement the crunchy watermelon.

600 g watermelon, cut into bite-sized chunks, any black seeds removed
1 medium sized spring onion, sliced thinly on the bias
200 g feta or another sheep milk cheese, in large chunks
½ cup pitted oily black olives, such as Kalamata
5 mint leaves, finely chopped

Combine the watermelon, olives, and spring onions in a large bowl. Gently fold in the cheese, being careful to keep it in chunks. Sprinkle with the mint and serve immediately.

Pear, pomegranate and avocado salad

Recipe provided by **Farzana** from **Afghanistan**
Makes a side salad for 4

Farzana says pears grow abundantly in the higher altitude regions of Afghanistan. This beautifully simple salad teams them up with their creamy avocado cousins from the lower, warmer parts of the country. Don't forget to scatter with lots of pomegranate rubies!

4 handfuls mixed salad leaves
2 handfuls rocket
1 tablespoon sesame or olive oil
1 large dessert pear, cored and cut into thick slices
juice from ½ a lemon
1 teaspoon honey
1 large avocado, cut into slices similar in size to the pear
seeds from half a pomegranate
small handful of torn basil leaves
salt

Place the salad leaves in a large bowl. Set aside.

Heat the oil in a frying pan over medium-high heat. Add the pear and cook until they're golden brown and crispy (if you'd like to have the salad as a main dish for two consider using two pears). Leaving as much juice in the pan as possible, use a slotted spoon to transfer the pear slices to the greens.

While the oil is still hot, add the lemon juice and honey to the pan juices and whisk thoroughly to make a smooth dressing.

Arrange the avocado slices on top of the pear and drizzle the dressing overtop. Sprinkle with the pomegranate seeds, basil leaves, and season with a generous pinch of salt. Serve right away.

Epikairo!

Established in 2014, Epikairo is a family owned restaurant on Samos Island. Run by Monika, her husband Manolis and their daughters Yvonne and Georgia, Epikairo remains open through the winter, is very reasonably priced, and from the very beginning has been incredibly welcoming to refugees and volunteers alike.

Though originally from Poland, Monika has lived in Greece for 28 years and for that reason, she felt could relate to some of the feelings of the displaced community. Of her own arrival in Samos, she remembers feeling she had no past in Greece, yet no future in Poland – 'You are where you are and you make the best of it.'

She certainly has done! Epikairo is a firm favourite of those at Samos Volunteers. Due to its wonderful food and welcoming atmosphere it has been the destination of choice for weekly meetings, as well as warm welcome parties, fond farewells and celebrations of newly granted asylum.

Many refugees and volunteers have great memories of the restaurant and its excellent food. It was only right for this book to feature an Epikairo dish.

Salads

Monika's aubergine salad

Recipe provided by **Monika** from **Epikairo restaurant on Samos Island**
Makes a side salad for 8

2 large aubergines
½ teaspoon salt for
  rubbing
1 teaspoon olive oil
2 medium green peppers,
  sliced
1 medium red pepper,
  sliced
1 medium red onion,
  thinly sliced
2 ½ tablespoons roughly
  chopped flat leaf
  parsley
2 ½ tablespoons extra
  virgin olive oil
½ teaspoons salt
black pepper
juice of half a lemon
  or 1 tablespoon red
  wine vinegar

Preheat the oven to 160 °C, gas mark 3.

Using a fork, prick the skin of the aubergines
all over. Rub with the oil and salt, place in a
baking tin and cook in the center of the oven for
35-40 minutes. Remove and allow to cool.

Whilst the aubergine cools slice the peppers
lengthways at around half a centimetre wide.
Thinly slice the onion and combine with
the peppers and chopped parsley in a large
salad bowl.

Once cooled cut the aubergine into large chunks
2-3 cm thick and add to the bowl with the other
ingredients. Dress with extra virgin olive oil,
lemon juice, salt and pepper. Toss and serve.

Algerian pastilla

Recipe provided by **Nedjmaa** from **Algeria**
Serves 6

Nedjmaa is a young single mum with a severely disabled daughter, struggling with the conditions in the camp, but her face lit up with joy and nostalgia when describing pastilla – one of Algeria's beloved traditional dishes. Equally delicious are non-meat versions of this lovely light pie; you could use chestnuts, walnuts or green lentils mixed with spices and seasonal vegetables.

150 g butter, melted
1 large onion, finely chopped
1-2 inch piece fresh ginger, grated
2 garlic cloves, minced
1 tablespoon cinnamon, plus extra for dusting
¾ teaspoon ground cardamom
1 teaspoon ground turmeric
6 chicken breasts cut into thin slices
1 tablespoon plain white flour
500 ml chicken stock
100 g ground almonds
1 tablespoon runny honey
85 g chopped dried apricots
50 g toasted almond flakes
Small handful of chopped parsley
1 250 g packet filo pastry ▶

Heat 50 g of the butter in a large pan. Add the onion, ginger, and garlic and cook until the onions are soft.

Add the cinnamon, cardamom, and turmeric and fry gently for 30 seconds. Add the chicken to the pan in a single layer, turning once to brown both sides. Sprinkle the flour over top. Mix carefully, then add the stock slowly to avoid lumps. Simmer gently for 45 minutes. Use tongs to remove the chicken pieces to a plate, leaving the juices behind.

Stir the ground almonds and honey into the pan juices and simmer until the juices are reduced by half. Shred the chicken and return to the sauce, along with the apricots, almond flakes, parsley, and orange zest. The mixture should be quite thick. Leave to cool completely while you prep the cake tin.

Preheat your oven to 180 °C, gas mark 4, with a rack positioned in the centre.

Generously butter an 25 cm round cake tin. Brush 10 filo sheets carefully with the remaining ▶

zest of 1 medium orange
1 dessertspoon of icing
  sugar

butter and arrange in 5 overlapping layers in the base of the well-buttered tin. Let any extra filo flop over the sides.

Fill the lined tin with the cooled chicken mixture, then top with a further 4 overlapping layers of filo. Bring the layers of filo that are flopped over the sides of the tin back over the top layers of filo and scrunch the remaining layer to dot decoratively over the top.

Bake for 45 minutes, or until golden brown. Remove from the oven and let cool for ten minutes. Then, dust with the sugar and some more cinnamon before serving.

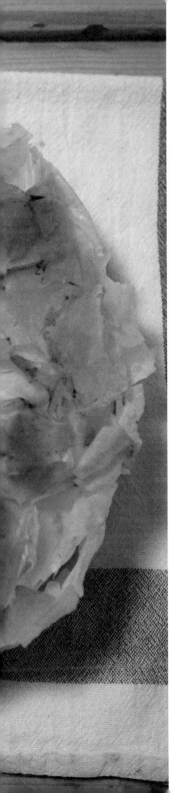

Chicken musakhan

Recipe provided by **Nora** from **Palestine**
Makes a side salad for 4

|| Considered by many to be the national dish of Palestine, musakhan
holds especially happy memories for Nora ,who would make it with her
grandmother every time there was a family birthday.

For the parcels

2 tablespoons olive oil, plus
more for brushing
1 kg boneless, skin-on
chicken thighs
3 medium white onions,
thinly sliced
1 whole dried chilli, seeds
removed if you'd like it
to be mild
100 g currants
100 ml pomegranate
molasses
240 ml water
6 thin flatbreads or tortilla
wraps, at least 20 cm
in diameter
sea salt

For the salad

2 small red onions, very
thinly sliced
2 teaspoons sumac
juice of 1/2 lemon
1 pomegranate, seeded
1 cup chopped fresh
parsley leaves
2 tablespoons olive oil ▶

Preheat the oven to 180°C, gas mark 4.

Make the filling:
Heat 2 tablespoons oil in a large frying pan over medium heat. Season the chicken with 1 teaspoon salt and add to the pan skin-side down. Cook without disturbing for 10 minutes until skin is crisp and golden and the fat is rendered out. Flip the thighs over to brown the other side for 5 minutes.

Remove the chicken from the frying pan with a slotted spoon and place to one side in a dish. Add the white onion and 1 teaspoon salt to the frying pan. Toss to coat the onions in the chicken fat and fry on a medium heat until they soften and become transparent, 15 minutes.

Transfer both the chicken and the onions to a large baking tray. Stir in the chilli, currants, pomegranate molasses and water. Cover the tray with aluminium foil and bake in the oven until the chicken seperates and shreds easily with a fork, about 45 minutes.

Take the baking tray from the oven, remove and discard the dried chilli. Using two forks, shred the chicken. Once in bitesize strips, leave the mixture in the baking tray to cool. ▶

1 cup torn fresh mint
  leaves
sea salt and black pepper

Make the parcels:
Line a baking sheet with parchment paper or
aluminum foil. Place one flatbread in a soup bowl,
allowing the edges to hang over the rim of the
bowl. Fill with a sixth of the chicken filling, then
fold the sides in to seal like a package.

Place the parcel seam-side down on the prepared
baking sheet. Repeat with the remaining
flatbreads and filling. Brush each package with a
little olive oil, then bake for 10 to 15 minutes, until
the parcels are crisp and golden brown.

Make the salad:
Toss the onions, sumac, lemon juice, pomegranate
seeds, parsley, mint, and olive oil in a medium
bowl. Season to taste with salt and pepper. Serve
alongside the parcels.

Aushak

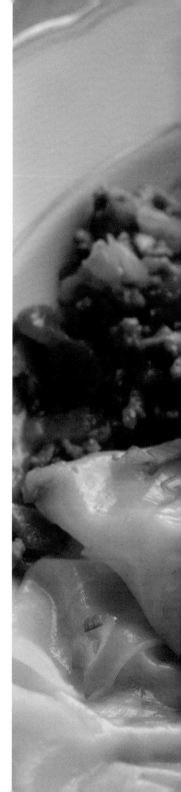

Recipe provided by **Farzana** from **Afghanistan**
Makes 10 dumplings

Farzana has very fond memories of eating
these wonderful dumplings back home in
Kabul when she was growing up. She and
her husband are hoping to make a new life
in London.

First, make the meat sauce. Heat the olive oil
in a large frying pan over medium-high heat.
Add the onions, garlic, ground coriander, ginger,
bay leaf, and 1 teaspoon salt and cook, stirring
often, until soft. Add the beef to the pan and
cook, stirring occasionally, until golden brown.
Add the tomatoes and fresh basil and cook on
low heat until the sauce has thickened and the
meat is tender. While the sauce cooks, assemble
the dumplings.

Bring a large pot of water to boil. While the water
comes to a boil, mix the spring onions, leeks,
jalapeño, garlic, and chilli flakes in a medium
bowl. Season with salt and pepper.

Place the wonton sheets on a cutting board and
brush the edges with water. Divide the filling
evenly between the sheets and cover with another
sheet, pressing the edges to seal.

Season the boiling water with salt and cook the
dumplings for 1 to 2 minutes, then drain. Dollop
some sauce in 4 shallow bowls. Top with 2 to 3
dumplings, then more sauce. Serve with yoghurt
and sprinkled with the reserved spring onions.

For the sauce
2 tablespoons olive oil
1 bay leaf
sea salt
3 medium onions, finely
   chopped
3 garlic cloves, finely
   chopped
450 g beef mince
2½ teaspoons ground
   coriander
1 tablespoon finely
   chopped fresh ginger
1 400 g can chopped tinned
   tomatoes
1 large sprig fresh basil

For the dumplings
7 spring onions, some
   reserved for serving
2 leeks, halved and finely
   sliced
1 jalapeño pepper, finely
   chopped
1 garlic clove, finely
   chopped
1 teaspoon chilli flakes
sea salt and black pepper
20 wonton wrappers
plain yoghurt, for serving

59

Misir Wot

Recipe provided by **Djamila** from **Djibouti**
Serves 4 accompanied with bread and salad

Djamila gave us this recipe to a fiery favourite of hers: Misir Wot. It is a thick and hearty lentil dish that packs a punch thanks to the traditional Berbere spices. It is a real comfort food and perfect scooped up with plenty of Laxoox (see recipe page 18).

Make the Berbere spice mix:
Heat a frying pan over a medium heat. When the pan is hot, dry fry the coriander seeds, cumin, fenugreek, allspice, clove, cardamom and dried chilli for 3 minutes or until the seeds start to bounce and pop a little. Transfer to a spice grinder or pestle and mortar, and grind the fried spices into a coarse powder. Put the mixture into a bowl and add the sweet paprika, cinnamon and turmeric. Mix well and put aside.

Make the lentils:
In a heavy bottomed saucepan, over a medium heat, cook the lentils in 2 cups of water. Cook for 30 minutes stirring occasionally. Add a little more water if they get too dry or sticky. Once the water has been absorbed and the lentils are soft, remove from the heat and set to one side.

Heat the oil in a frying pan over a medium heat. Add the onions and fry gently for 15 minutes until translucent. Add the garlic and ginger and fry for a further 10 minutes until all ingredients in the pan are soft. Add the Berbere spice mix to the onion, garlic and ginger, stirring quickly to coat them in the spices. Add the remaining ½ cup of water and allow to simmer for 5 minutes.

Transfer the spiced onion, garlic and ginger mixture from the frying pan to the saucepan of lentils. Stir through thoroughly and return the saucepan to a medium heat for a further ten minutes until the lentils have a thick and creamy consistency.

Serve with plenty of delicious Laxoox (see recipe page 18) and a green salad.

For the Berbere spice mix
1 teaspoon coriander seeds
1 teaspoon cumin
$\frac{1}{2}$ teaspoon fenugreek
   seeds
1 allspice berry
1 clove
seeds of 2 green
   cardomom pods
1 $\frac{1}{2}$ dried red chilli
   (or to taste)
1 $\frac{1}{2}$ tablespoon sweet
   paprika
$\frac{1}{2}$ teaspoon cinnamon
$\frac{1}{2}$ teaspoon turmeric

For the lentils
250 g red lentils
2$\frac{1}{2}$ cups water
1 tablespoon olive oil
1 large onion, finely
   chopped
3 cloves of garlic minced
2 cm fresh ginger finely
   chopped
1 teaspoon salt

*Berbere is used as the basis
for many Djiboutian and
Ethiopian stews this fiery
spice mix is delicious and
keeps very well. Double up
on the quantities and keep
the leftover mix in a jam
jar for future dishes.

Syrian lamb with green bean

Recipe provided by **Amal** from **Syria**
Serves 6

Amal and his wife save this succulent stew for annual family gatherings and say it is best made two days in advance. The dark, rich gravy contrasts beautifully with the vibrant green of the beans. If preparing in advance, the secret is to blanch the beans separately and add to the meat just before re-heating and serving. Wonderful with couscous or steamed rice.

3 tablespoons olive oil
2 large onions, chopped
4 large cloves of garlic, minced
1 tablespoon ras el hanout paste or 1 dessertspoon ras el hanout powder
700 g trimmed lamb shoulder meat in cubes
2 red peppers, cut into 1 inch pieces
350 g French beans, topped and tailed
450 g cherry tomatoes
500 ml stock
a generous handful of mixed basil and mint, chopped
plain rice and/or lavash bread for serving

Heat the oil in a large frying pan. Add the onion, garlic, ras el hanout, and 1 teaspoon each of salt and pepper. Cook, stirring often, until the onions are soft, 10 to 15 minutes. Use a slotted spoon to remove the onions to a plate, leaving the oil behind in the pan.

Return the pan to medium-high heat. Season the lamb with 1 teaspoon each of salt and pepper and cook until browned, 10 minutes. Add the reserved onions and garlic to the pan, along with the red pepper, green beans (not if cooking in advance, see above), and tomatoes. Pour on just enough stock to cover the meat. Cover and simmer gently for 1 hour, or until the meat is really tender.

Top with the basil and mint and serve with rice and/or lavash bread.

For the vegetables

¼ cup olive oil

4 cloves garlic, minced

2 tablespoons ground
  coriander

2 teaspoons salt

2 medium aubergines,
  halved and sliced
  1 cm thick

2 red peppers, sliced
  1 cm thick

2 red onions, sliced
  1 cm thick

For the rice

2 cups short grain rice,
  rinsed until the water
  runs clear

2½ cups water

1 teaspoon salt

For the spinach

50 g unsalted butter

1 bay leaf

1 cinnamon stick

½ teaspoon ground
  cardamom

750 g spinach leaves

1 cup vegetable stock

2 teaspoons lemon juice

Mollocan spiced vegetables

Recipe provided by **Shayma** from **Kuwait**
Serves 8 as a side

Unusually for a Kuwaiti, Shayma is a vegetarian and has been from a very young age. Mollocan, as Shayma calls it, is a green vegetable grown in the Middle East, often written as Mulukhiya or Molokkia. It's much harder to find in Western Europe and so Shayma has started to make the dish with spinach. She says that the flavour is slightly different but it's a very good substitute.

Roast the vegetables:
Preheat your oven to 200°C, gas mark 6. In a large mixing bowl, stir the olive oil, garlic, coriander, and salt until you get a paste. Add the chopped vegetables and toss until well coated. Divide the vegetables between two rimmed baking trays. Roast for about 30 minutes until the aubergine is tender and golden brown, rotating the sheets front to back and top to bottom halfway through cooking.

Cook the rice:
Soak the rice for 30 minutes. Drain and combine with the $2^{1}/_{2}$ cups water in a thick-bottomed pan. Bring to a boil on high heat, then reduce to a very gentle simmer and cover. Cook 10 minutes, remove from the heat, and let steam 5 minutes. Fluff with a fork.

Sauté the spinach:
In a wide, high-sided pan, melt the butter over medium-high heat. Add the bay leaf, cinnamon stick, and cardamom. Fry for 2 to 3 minutes, stirring often, until fragrant. Add the spinach, stock, and lemon juice. Stir to coat the spinach in the spiced butter, then cover and cook until the spinach wilts, about 2 minutes.

To serve, pile the rice in a large serving bowl. Top with the spinach and then the vegetables. Eat hot.

Kofta

Recipe provided by **Mansour** from **Egypt**
Makes 30 bitesized kofta

Mansour gave us this version of the much loved spicy meatball;
he says they're eaten in his family on a practically daily basis. Perfect
as a sandwhich in some crusty bread with some roasted peppers!

450 g finely minced lamb
1 onion, finely chopped
2 cloves garlic, crushed
2 tablespoons finely
  chopped parsley
2 tablespoons finely
  chopped mint
2 teaspoons ground cumin
1 teaspoon sumac
  (optional)
salt and pepper

Combine the lamb, onion, garlic, parsley, mint,
cumin, sumac (if using), and 1 teaspoon each
salt and pepper in a large bowl. Mix thoroughly
but gently with your hands and form into bite-
sized balls.

To cook, either thread three or four onto a skewer
and grill for 3 minutes on each side, or cook
gently in olive oil until brown and crispy and
cooked through.

Kibbeh

Recipe provided by **Neddah** from **Syria**
Makes 24 Kibbeh

Kibbeh is a Levantine dish originally made with camel meat. Neddah and her family from Kurdish Syria always make it with lamb accompanied by lots of traditional spices. According to Neddah, the true authentic Kibbeh must always be shaped 'like pointed torpedoes' – amazing what you can find out with Google Translate!

For the filling
1 tablespoon olive oil
1 medium onion,
  finely chopped
250 g lamb mince
½ teaspoon ground allspice
¼ teaspoon cinnamon
salt and pepper
½ cup pine nuts, toasted

For the dough
1½ cups fine bulgur wheat
2 cups stock, heated
700 g lamb mince
1 large onion, quartered
½ cup chopped mint leaves
2 teaspoons cumin
½ teaspoon ground allspice
salt and pepper
750 ml neutral oil, such as
  sunflower or canola oil,
  for frying

For the tomato sauce
and to serve
400 g cherry tomatoes ▶

Make the filling:
Heat the oil in a large frying pan over medium-high heat. Add the onions and cook until soft. Add the meat and cook until brown. Stir in the allspice, cinnamon, 1 teaspoon each salt and pepper and cook for 4 more minutes. Stir in the pinenuts and let cool while you make the dough.

Make the dough:
Soak the bulgur in the stock for 30 minutes. Drain and squeeze out any excess stock. Transfer to the bowl of a food processor and add the meat, onion, mint, cumin, allspice, 1 teaspoon salt, and ½ teaspoon pepper. Process until a smooth paste forms.

Assemble and cook kibbeh:
To form the kibbeh croquettes, shape the dough into egg-sized balls. Using your thumb, hollow out the egg shape to form a thin walled oval. Fill the hole with a teaspoon of the filling, then enclose it by pressing the dough around the centre to form a rugby ball shaped croquette. Press firmly between hands to totally seal in the filling with the dough. ▶

1 tablespoon olive oil
handful fresh basil leaves
½ teaspoon smoked
  paprika
salt and pepper
Greek yoghurt, lemon
  wedges, mint leaves,
  for serving

Heat the oil in a shallow, straight-sided pan fitted with a deep-frying thermometer until the oil reaches 180 °C. Fry the kibbeh in batches, until golden brown and cooked through, about 8 minutes total. Use a long-handled, shallow spoon to turn the dumpling over so it browns evenly on all sides. Transfer to a paper towel lined plate and repeat with remaining croquettes.

Make the sauce:
Heat the oil in a frying pan over medium heat. Add the tomatoes, basil, and paprika and cook, stirring often, until the tomatoes are soft and squidgy, 10 to 15 minutes.

Serve alongside the kibbeh with the yoghurt, mint, and lemon wedges.

Lahmajoun

Recipe provided by **Rupelina** from **Syria**
Makes 8, 30 cm Lahmajoun

Rupelina is a young mum of three from
Kurdish Syria, desperately missing the cuisine
of her homeland. She describes Lahmajoun
as a Middle Eastern version of pizza. Her
favourite food, it's easily adapted to both meat
and vegetarian toppings and is really easy and
fun to make.

Make the dough:
Combine all the ingredients in a large mixing
bowl and knead until a sticky but not wet dough
forms. Cover with a damp cloth and set in a warm
place until the dough has doubled in size, about
1 hour.

Meanwhile, make the filling. Transfer all
the ingredients in a large mixing bowl until
thoroughly combined.

Divide the risen dough into 8 parts and roll out
on a floured surface into 20 to 25 cm disks. They
should be about 2 to 3 mm thick. Transfer the
dough rounds to parchment paper, and spread
each one with ½ cup of the lamb filling. Spread
almost all the way to the edges. Let rise until
doubled in thickness, about 30 minutes more.
While the dough rises, preheat the oven to 180 °C,
gas mark 4.

Bake until the dough is golden brown and crispy,
18 to 22 minutes. Sprinkle with flaky sea salt,
parsley leaves and lemon juice. Eat hot.

For the dough
1 kg flour
2½ cups of lukewarm
    water
1 tablespoon instant yeast
1 teaspoon salt
1 teaspoon sugar
1 tablespoon of olive oil

For the lamb mixture
500 g minced lamb
2 medium red onions,
    finely chopped
500 g peeled and finely
    chopped tomatoes
1 red pepper, finely
    chopped
3 cloves of garlic, minced
2 tablespoons tomato paste
1 tablespoon Aleppo
    pepper flakes
1 tablespoon smoked
    paprika
1 tablespoon salt
½ tablespoon ground
    black pepper

fresh lemon wedges and
    flaky sea salt, for serving

Samak maqli

Recipe provided by **Yasmin** from **Syria**
Serves 4

Yasmin from Aleppo gladly shared this recipe of fried fish, soft tomatoes and a sumptuous herb sauce. She says it brings back many happy memories of childhood trips to the Syrian coastal town of Latakia where her family would enjoy long and leisurely lunches of freshly caught fish before heading off to her grandfather's orchard nearby to spend the afternoon sleeping it off under the pomegranate trees.

Half an hour before cooking, rub the fish with the cumin and salt.

Make the herb sauce:
Combine the finely chopped herbs, lemon juice, honey, garlic and olive oil. Stir well and season to taste with the salt and pepper. Set aside.

Make the fish:
Over a high heat, heat the sunflower oil in a thick bottomed frying pan. It should cover the bottom of the pan to around 1cm depth. Whilst the oil heats up dredge each fish fillet in flour, covering both sides. Carefully place the fish into the hot oil, it should immediately start to crackle. Fry for 6-7 mins, turning the fillets halfway through. If there isn't enough space to fit all the fish in the pan comfortably then fry in batches. Once crisp and golden brown remove the fish from the pan and onto a plate lined with kitchen towel.

Make the Tomatoes:
While the fish is cooking roll the plum tomatoes in olive oil and salt in a bowl, coating them evenly. Heat a frying pan with a lid over a medium heat. Once the pan is hot add the tomatoes and fry covered for 10-12 minutes, shaking the pan every couple of minutes until the tomatoes are soft and their skins are beginning to char and bruise. Add the parsley and oregano, give the pan another good shake, turn off the heat and season.

Drizzle the herb sauce over the crisp, fried fish and serve with the warm tomatoes as an accompaniment.

For the fish
4 fillets of firm white fish
    (cod, haddock or bream)
1½ teaspoons ground
    cumin
½ teaspoon salt
3 tablespoons plain white
    flour
100 ml sunflower oil
    for frying

For the herb sauce
½ cup finely chopped flat
    leaf parsley
½ cup finely chopped
    coriander
2 tablespoons lemon juice
1 teaspoon honey
1 large clove of garlic,
    crushed
3 tablespoons extra virgin
    olive oil
salt and black pepper

For the tomatoes
300 g plum tomatoes
2 tablespoons olive oil
1 tablespoon roughly
    chopped flat leaf parsley
1 tablespoon roughly
    chopped oregano
salt and black pepper

Ali's garlic mashed potatoes

Recipe provided by **Ali** from **Syria**
Serves 4 as a side

|| Ali from Aleppo is one of Samos Volunteers' much valued and
appreciated Community Volunteers. A fluent English speaker, Ali teaches
Greek alphabet at one of the many classes at the Alpha Community
Centre. He says this delicious garlicky mash is his perfect comfort food.

**For the mashed
potatoes**
3 large floury potatoes,
  such as Russet, peeled
3 large eggs
1 tablespoon olive oil
¼ teaspoon chilli powder
salt and pepper
¼ cup chopped parsley
  to garnish

For the sauce
1 cup plain yoghurt
1 garlic clove, minced
1 small cucumber
1 tablespoon chopped
  mint leaves

Bring a large pot of water to a boil. Add the
potatoes and eggs and return to a boil. Use tongs
to remove the eggs after 10 minutes. Run them
under cold water or dunk in a bowl of ice water,
then peel, dry, and coarsely chop (saving 1 wedge
for a garnish). Set the eggs aside.

Cook the potatoes until you can easily insert a
dinner knife through the centre, 15 to 20 minutes.
Transfer the potatoes to a large bowl and mash
until very smooth. Stir in the chopped eggs, olive
oil, chilli powder, salt and pepper to taste. Garnish
with the parsley.

In a separate bowl, mix the yoghurt, finely
chopped cucumber and crushed garlic. Garnish
with the chopped mint leaves and serve alongside
the potatoes.

Spiced chickpeas

Recipe provided by **Zaha** from **Iraq**
Serves 4

|| This way of cooking chickpeas is a much loved family recipe given to us
by Zaha from Baghdad. One of those dishes that is almost more delicious
the day after being made.

$1/4$ cup olive oil
1 large onion, finely
chopped
4 cloves garlic, minced
1 tablespoon ground
coriander
1 teaspoon grated fresh
ginger
$1/2$ teaspoon ground cumin
$1/2$ teaspoon ground
cinnamon
1 450 g tin diced tomatoes
450 g cooked chickpeas
– equivalent to around
2 drained 400 g tins
$1/4$ teaspoon ground cloves
$1/2$ teaspoon ground
cayenne
pinch sugar (optional)
$1/2$ cup finely chopped
mixed fresh parsley and
mint leaves
pita bread and labneh
or Greek yoghurt,
for serving

Heat the olive oil in a large frying pan over
medium heat, add the onion and cook until
starting to soften, 10 minutes. Add the garlic,
coriander, ginger, cumin, and cinnamon. Cook
until the onions are completely soft and fragrant.
Stir in the tomatoes and cook for a further
5 minutes, then add the chickpeas, cloves, cayenne
and $1/2$ teaspoon each salt and pepper. Continue
to cook for another 10-15 minutes until the
mixture becomes thick and pulpy and the spices
have become more rounded in flavour. If needed,
continue to season to taste with salt and pepper,
and add a little sugar if the spices have become
at all bitter.

If serving immediately, pile on a platter and
spread with the parsley and mint, or pile into
pita bread pockets with a dollop of labneh or
Greek yoghurt.

Freekeh

Recipe provided by **Fairuza** from **Iran**
Serves 2 as a main and 4 as a side

> Freekeh is a delicious green wheat with a
> distinctive nutty taste, harvested while the
> grains are still soft and then sundried. This
> salad from Fairuza is crunchy, spicy, tart
> and fruity all at the same time. It is a meal
> in itself and infinitely adaptable to whatever
> ingredients you have in your store cupboard.

Bring the stock to a boil in a large pan. Add
the freekeh and 1 teaspoon salt. Reduce to a
simmer and cook until tender but still crunchy,
about 20 minutes. If the level of liquid gets
low, you might need to add some more stock.

Meanwhile, heat the olive oil in a large frying
pan over medium heat. Add the onion and
garlic and cook until starting to soften. Stir
in the ginger, coriander, cardamom, and
½ teaspoon salt. Cook, stirring often, until
the onion is soft. Fold in the orange zest.

Drain the freekeh and transfer to a large bowl.
Fold in the onion and spiced mixture, then
add the walnuts, carrot, half the pomegranate
seeds, mixed seeds (if using). Gently fold in
the basil, adjust the seasoning as needed, and
top with the remaining pomegranate seeds.

2 cups vegetable stock
150 g freekeh*, washed and
  drained twice
salt and pepper
3 tablespoons olive oil
1 medium onion, finely
  chopped
2 garlic cloves, mashed
1 tablespoon grated fresh
  ginger
1 teaspoon ground
  coriander
½ teaspoon ground
  cardamom
zest of 1 small orange
120 g walnuts, toasted and
  roughly chopped
1 medium carrot, finely
  grated
seeds from a medium
  pomegranate
handful of mixed seeds,
  such as sunflower or
  sesame seeds (optional)
1 large handful torn
  basil leaves

*Freekeh requires two
rounds of washing and
draining to remove
any grit or residue. You
can find it in health
food shops and in large
supermarkets. It's full
of flavour and makes a
wonderful alternative to
rice or couscous.

Qabuli pilau

Recipe provided by **Farzana** from **Afghanistan**
Serves 8

> This dish is widely considered to be the national dish of Afghanistan.
> Served on special occasions using only the very best of ingredients
> Farzana, who told us all about this dish, has very happy memories of
> sitting down with her family in Kabul and enjoying the fun, food and
> holiday atmosphere.

For the meat
2 tablespoons olive oil
1 medium onion, finely
   chopped
2 large garlic cloves,
   minced
salt and pepper
500 g lamb shoulder, diced
   in roughly 5 cm pieces
¾ cup stock

**For the carrot and
raisin mixture**
3 tablespoons vegetable oil
2 carrots, grated
¼ cup water
1½ teaspoons sugar
½ cup raisins

**For the caramelised
sauce and rice**
500 g basmati rice,
   soaked at least 4 hours
   or overnight
1½ tablespoons salt
2 tablespoons sugar ▶

Cook the meat:
Heat the oil in a large frying pan over medium
heat. Add the onion, garlic, and 1 teaspoon
salt. Cook, stirring often, until the onions are
soft. Add the lamb, and 1 teaspoon each salt
and pepper. Cook, turning the pieces of lamb
occasionally, until browned, 10 to 15 minutes.
Add the stock and stir to make sure everything
is evenly distributed. Set aside.

Make the carrot and raisin mixture:
Heat half the oil in a frying pan over medium
heat. Add the carrots, water, and sugar and
cook until softened. Transfer to a bowl and
return the pan to the heat. Add the remaining
half of the oil and the raisins. Cook until they
swell up, 5 to 10 minutes. Return the carrots to
the pan and mix well. Set aside.

Make the rice and caramel sauce:
Bring a large saucepan of water to a boil and
add the rice and salt. Cook for ten minutes,
then drain and return the rice to the saucepan.
Set aside. In a separate, clean, dry saucepan,
cook the sugar over medium-high heat. Do not
stir and keep a careful eye, watching ▶

¼ cup oil
½ cup stock
1½ teaspoons ground
  cumin
parsley, to serve

as the sugar liquefies and turns a golden brown caramel colour. Remove from the heat and very carefully add the oil – it will cause a crackling noise. Stir furiously and then add the stock, salt, and cumin, stirring constantly. Return the mixture to the heat and boil for 2 minutes. Pour the caramelised sauce over the rice and stir to coat evenly. Smooth the coated rice into an even layer at the bottom of the saucepan, then use the end of a clean wooden spoon to poke holes throughoutso it will steam evenly.

Cook everything together:
Top the rice with the meat mixture, then top with the carrots and raisins. Cover the saucepan with a a clean tea towel, then cook over low heat for 30 to 35 minutes.

To serve, cover the base of a platter with a little rice, then top with the lamb, followed by the remaining rice before garnishing with the carrot and raisins. Sprinkle with the chopped parsley and season with salt and pepper.

Tigadegena

Recipe provided by Abdoulaye from Mali
Serves 6

Tigadegena is a peanut stew from Mali. Abdoulaye explained that Tigadegena should be eaten with freshly cooked rice that is crumbly and soft. He says that everyone from Mali knows this dish and it is his favourite meal from home.

2 tablespoons vegetable oil

700g thickly diced stewing beef or lamb

3 medium onions, finely diced

5 cloves of garlic, finely chopped or pressed

4 large tomatoes, diced

2 green peppers, chopped roughly into 2cm squares

½ cabbage (Savoy goes well), roughly chopped

200g okra, topped, tailed and cut roughly into 2cm lengths

1 teaspoon salt

5 tbsp peanut butter

500ml boiling water

50g roughly chopped peanuts to garnish

Heat the oil in a large stewing pot or casserole over a medium to high heat. Add the meat and brown it on all sides for 5 to 7 minutes.

Once the meat is browned, add the onions and garlic and cook for a further 7 to 10 minutes until the onions are soft and translucent. Add the remainder of the vegetables and the salt, and fry together for a further 5 minutes.

In a separate, heatproof mixing jug, dissolve the peanut butter into the boiling water. Pour the mixture over the vegetables and meat. Stir well. Reduce the heat to low and put a lid on the pot or casserole.

Leave the mixture to simmer for an hour and a half. Stir occasionally and gradually add more water if the stew starts to get dry. Season or swirl in a little more peanut butter to taste. Serve with rice and garnish with the roughly chopped peanuts.

Almond falafel

Recipe provided by **Amran** from **Syria**
Makes 16-18 falafel

A crunchy version of an old favourite, contributed by Amran. Great dipped in thick yoghurt or labneh which has been sprinkled with dukkah (see recipe page 20).

2 tablespoons olive oil
1 large onion, finely chopped
4 garlic cloves, minced
1 teaspoon chilli flakes
1 teaspoon ground cumin
1 teaspoon salt
1 400 g tin chickpeas, drained and warmed, or ½ cup soaked and freshly cooked chickpeas, still hot
2 tablespoons chopped fresh coriander
2 tablespoons chopped fresh flat leaf parsley
1 teaspoon baking powder
½ cup finely chopped toasted almonds
⅓ cup plain white flour
1 litre sunflower or vegetable oil, for frying

Heat the oil in a frying pan over medium-high heat. Add the onion, garlic, chilli flakes, cumin, and 1 teaspoon salt. Cook, stirring often, until the onion is soft, 12 to 14 minutes.

Transfer the onion to a blender or Magimix, and add the hot chickpeas, coriander, parsley, and baking powder. Stir to combine everything well, add the almonds, and then pulse blend until the mixture has a coarse, consistent, lump free texture. Transfer from the blender to a bowl, cover and refrigerate for at least 1 hour and up to overnight.

When you're ready to cook, heat the vegetable oil in a shallow, straight-sided pan fitted with a deep-frying thermometer until the oil reaches 180 °C.

While the oil heats, shape the falafel. Place the flour in a shallow bowl. Use wet hands to shape 1 tablespoon of mixture into balls. Roll them in the flour and then fry the falafel in batches, until golden brown and crispy on the outside, about 4 minutes total. Transfer cooked falafel to paper towel lined plates. Serve hot.

Mejadra
spiced lentils

Recipe provided by **Afsaneh** from **Iran**
Serves 6 as a side

Afsaneh from Tabriz in Iran gave us the recipe for this national favourite. It's a little time consuming to make but well worth the effort especially for fans of vegan cuisine. Afsaneh remembers her siblings fighting over who got the crispy fried onions on top.

Make the lentils and rice:
Heat the oil, cumin, and coriander gently in a large saucepan over medium heat until the spices are fragrant, about 3 minutes. Add the rice, stirring to coat with the oil and spices. Fry gently for 1 or 2 minutes.

Add the stock and lentils and bring to a boil. Add the cinnamon, turmeric, sugar, and 1 teaspoon each salt and pepper. Reduce to a gentle simmer, cover, and cook for 15 minutes, until all the stock is absorbed. Set the mixture aside while you cook the onions.

Make the onions:
Heat the oil in a large, straight-sided frying pan until almost smoking. Dust the onion slices with a little flour. Fry quickly in batches until golden brown and crispy, 3 to 4 minutes. Transfer to a paper towel-lined plate to absorb excess oil and sprinkle with salt.

To serve, stir two thirds of the onions into the lentil-rice mixture, transfer to a large serving bowl and sprinkle the remaining crispy onions on top.

For the lentils
2 tablespoons olive oil
1 ½ tablespoons ground
   coriander
1 tablespoon ground cumin
1 cup basmati rice
2 cups vegetable stock
1 400 g tin cooked brown
   lentils, or an equivalent
   home-cooked amount
½ tablespoons ground
   cinnamon
½ teaspoon ground
   turmeric
1 teaspoon sugar
salt and pepper

For the onions
3 large onions, thinly sliced
40 g plain flour for dusting
250 ml sunflower or
   vegetable oil
salt

Pomegranate and halva ice cream

Recipe provided by **Roholla** from **Afghanistan**
Makes 1 litre of ice cream.

This recipe is a delicious consequence of an animated discussion at Samos Volunteers' Alpha Centre. A student in one of the English classes had asked what 'Eton Mess' was – he'd seen it online. After it was demystified (adding Meringue to the vocabulary list along the way), everyone was soon discussing their home countries' equivalent. Roholla put forward his Mum's recipe for Afghani ice cream.

2 large pomegranates
1 tablespoon lemon juice
3 tablespoons honey
1 tablespoon caster sugar
1½ tablespoons vodka*
300 ml double cream
125 g halva
2 tablespoons roughly
   chopped pistachios

*Roholla is from a Muslim country and wouldn't have recommended using alcohol in this recipe. However, it is included here as an option as it has no taste, stops ice crystals forming and gives a smoother finish.

Remove all the seeds from the pomegranates. The easiest, mess-free method is to quarter them in the sink and then bend the quarters, prying the seeds out into a bowl. Keep aside 1 tablespoon of seeds for decoration. Blitz the remaining seeds with a food processor and then sieve, keeping just the juice (200-250 ml). Add the lemon juice, honey, sugar and vodka (if using) and stir well.

In a large mixing bowl whip the double cream until it's thick and smooth. It should double in volume. Slowly pour the juice mixture into the cream and then gradually crumble in the halva. Fold until you have a smooth and beautifully pink mixture. Taste and add a little more honey or lemon if needed. Pour the mixture into a container and leave for at least 6 hours in the freezer. When ready, scoop into bowls or tumblers and top with the extra pomegranate seeds and chopped pistachios to serve.

The original recipe calls
for labneh – a kind of
concentrated yoghurt,
difficult to find in many
European countries. Its use
avoids having to freeze the
mixture. Double cream is
used here as an alternative.

Konafa

Recipe provided by **Aliya** from **Iraq**
Makes one 30 cm cake

This is Aliya's favourite way to finish a meal. A very, very rich dessert beloved all over the Middle East and in many Eastern European countries, where it has a variety of different names. Perfect with a cup of strong espresso!

For the syrup
300 g granulated sugar
250 ml of cold water
juice of 1 lemon

For the pastry
450 g Konafa pastry*
200 g melted butter, plus
  more for the tin
½ teaspoon pure vanilla
  extract
75 g blanched whole
  almonds
2½ tablespoons granulated
  sugar
2 teaspoons ground
  cinnamon
400g soft ricotta cheese

*Konafa is used interchangeably to refer to both this delicious dessert as a whole and the pastry from which it's made. The stringy filo (also known as Kanafeh) can be bought in Turkish and Arabic ▶

Make the syrup:
Combine the sugar, water, and lemon juice in a heavy-bottomed sauce pan. Bring to a boil over high heat, then lower to a gentle simmer and reduce until syrupy. Cool to room temperature.

For the pastry:
Preheat the oven to 180 °C, gas mark 4, with a rack set in the centre.

Butter a 30 cm wide cake tin with 5 cm high sides. Arrange the almonds decoratively on the bottom of the cake tin. Set aside.

Place the Konafa pastry in a large bowl. Pour the melted butter over the pastry, using a fork to separate the strands, coating them evenly. Press half of the pastry gently on top of the almonds in the tin. Stir the vanilla extract and ricotta together until smooth and gently spread evenly over the pastry. Mix 2½ tablespoons granulated sugar with the cinnamon and sprinkle evenly over the ricotta. Top with the remaining buttered Konafa. Press down gently but firmly.

Bake in the centre of the oven until ▶

food shops as well as in large supermarkets.

golden brown, about 45 minutes. Remove from the oven and immediately pour the lemon flavoured syrup over top. Slide a knife around the edge of the tin to loosen the sides. Let cool to room temperature.

Once cooled, upturn the pastry onto a serving plate and gently remove the tin to reveal the almonds now on top.

The Sultan's shortbread

Recipe provided by **Ruth** from **Palestine**
Makes 18 small slices

|| This has got to be the best biscuit/cake in the world! Ruth who gave us this recipe has a lot of extra kilos to answer for. Well, we have to test all the recipes and we had to test this one four times to make sure it was OK.

Make the shortbread:
Preheat your oven to 160°C, gas mark 3, with a rack set in the centre. Butter and line a 22 by 32 cm tin and line with parchment paper.

Combine all the ingredients for the shortbread in a large bowl. Beat together for about 5 minutes until you have a smooth dough. Use your fingers to press the mixture evenly into the base of the lined tin. Use a smooth tumbler coated in flour to roll the surface of the dough so it's even. Prick all over with a fork and then bake until golden brown, about 25 minutes. Let cool.

Make the filling:
Stir the halva and tahini in a small bowl and then spread evenly over the cooked and cooled shortbread.

Make the caramel topping:
Combine the sugar and water in a saucepan. Dissolve over low heat, then bring to a gentle boil and cook, swirling gently here and there, until you have a deep, golden brown caramel, 10 to 12 minutes. Remove from the heat and, avoiding splashes, carefully add the butter and cream. Whisk until the butter has melted and everything is well combined, then stir in the tahini and pomegranate molasses (if using), and salt. Pour the caramel over the halva-tahini topping and smooth with a spatula.

Let cool for several hours, then cut into bars and sprinkle with sea salt.

For the shortbread
250 g unsalted butter,
  softened
100 g caster sugar
250 g plain flour
50 g cornflour
1 teaspoon cinammon
½ teaspoon salt

For the filling
400 g crumbled halva*
175 g tahini

For the caramel topping
250 g caster sugar
160 ml water
130 g unsalted butter, cubed
120 ml double cream
200 g tahini
2 teaspoons pomegranate
  molasses (optional)
1 teaspoon salt
flaky sea salt, for sprinkling

*Halva is a dense, pale paste
usually made of ground
sesame seeds, sugar and egg
white. It is eaten all over
the Middle East in different
variations. You can buy it at
Middle Eastern or Turkish
food shops and in the
international food sections
of large supermarkets.

Vitumbua mchele

Recipe provided by **Adams** from **Burundi**
Makes 40 bitesize vitumbua mchele or 20 cupcakes

Found in various forms throughout East Africa, vitumbua are small, delicately spiced, coconut and rice flour cakes. Adams texted his Mum back in Burundi to get this recipe. He says these are one of his favourite Burundian dishes but should be approached with caution due to their highly addictive nature! Delicious as a breakfast, or combined with some fruit coulis or plain yoghurt for dessert.

1 ½ cups short grain rice or 1¾ cups rice flour
400 ml can coconut milk
60 g sugar
½ tablespoon cornflour
½ teaspoon of salt
1 teaspoon of cardomom powder
1½ teaspoon instant yeast
2 teaspoon coconut oil for cooking
20 g icing sugar for dusting (optional)

We highly recommend the traditional method of using rice as it achieves the most flavoursome and textured results but if you're pushed for time you can substitute with rice flour. Just skip the first step.

Soak the rice for at least 4 hours, preferably overnight. After it has soaked, strain thoroughly with a sieve. Line a large baking tray with kitchen towel and spread the drained rice evenly across the flat tray. Leave rice to dry out for 30 minutes to 1 hour.

Once dried off, place the rice into a blender. Add the coconut milk, sugar, cornflour, salt, cardamom and yeast to the blender and pulse blend until you have a smooth consistency with no lumps.

Transfer the mixture to a bowl, cover and leave for 45 minutes to an hour in a warm, dry place. If using rice flour, simply mix it with the rest of the ingredients in a large bowl and cover for the same time. After it has rested, the mixture should be slightly bubbly. ▶

Heat a Vitumbua or Aebelskiver pan (see note) on a low-medium heat. Apply a little coconut oil to the cooking area of the pan. If your pan is nonstick you won't need much. Put 1 tablespoon of the mixture into each of the pan's holes, or until they're ¾ full. Cook for 4-5 minutes until you're able to flip the vitumbua using chopsticks or a cocktail stick. The batter in the middle will pour out a little as you turn them, but don't worry, this forms the second half of their spherical shape. Once turned, cook for a further 3 minutes. Transfer the vitumbua to a cooling rack and repeat with the next batch, using kitchen roll to wipe the pan of any excess dried batter between rounds. Once they've cooled, pile onto a plate, dust with the icing sugar and watch them disappear.

If you don't have a vitumbua pan, you can bake the mixture as cupcakes. Arrange 20 regular sized cupcake casings in a cupcake tray. Transfer 2 tablespoons of the mixture to each casing. Bake for 15-20 minutes until the top of the cake is turning golden brown. Allow to cool on a rack before serving.

Note
Vitumbua is also the name of the traditional pan used to cook these treats. It is made of cast iron and has multiple concave indents for cooking. It is very similar to the pan used to make the Scandinavian cakes Aebelskiver, which can also be used for this recipe. It's possible to buy either Vitumbua or Aebelskiver pans online at a reasonable price, but if you can't get one you can easily use the batter to make cupcakes or even fry it as a pancake.

Sheer brinj rice pudding

Recipe provided by **Farzana** from **Afghanistan**
Serves 4

Delicately scented with the very best rosewater, this delicious creamy Afghan version of rice pudding can be served piping hot with thin slices of medjool dates and a drizzle of honey, or cool from the fridge with poached apricots.

1 cup short grain white
   rice, rinsed
¼ teaspoon sea salt
2 cups water
2 cups single cream
2 cups whole milk
1 tablespoon rosewater
   (or to taste)
2 tablespoons honey

Bring the water to a boil in a medium saucepan over high heat. Add the salt and rice and reduce the heat to low. Cook for 20 minutes, until most of the water is absorbed.

Stir in the cream and milk and cook, stirring occasionally, for 45 to 50 minutes over low heat, until the pudding is thick and holds together in one mass when bubbling. Stir in the rosewater (if using) and honey.

Serve hot, or transfer to a glass bowl and refrigerate until cold.

Peaches with honey and rosemary syrup

Recipe provided by **Afsaneh** from **Iran**
Serves 4

This is a lovely, simple dessert that showcases the abundant fruits grown in the more temperate regions of Iran. Afsaneh, who contributed the recipe, says it provides a perfect finish to a meal of delicately spiced Persian cuisine.

4 big, juicy peaches cut into quarters
⅓ cup caster sugar
2 tablespoons honey
1 cup water
1 tablespoon lemon juice
4 sprigs fresh rosemary
1 teaspoon best quality rosewater (or to taste)
edible rose petals, for decorating (optional)

A few hours before serving, make the syrup. Combine the sugar, honey, water, lemon juice and rosemary in a small pan and bring to a gentle boil, stirring to make sure the sugar is dissolved. Boil 1 minute, then leave to stand for 1 hour. Strain into a clean jug to remove the rosemary leaves, then stir in the rosewater. Refrigerate until ready to use.

30 minutes before serving, gently toss the peaches and syrup in a large bowl, then pile into a serving bowl. Decorate with edible rose petals or a sprig of rosemary, if you'd like.

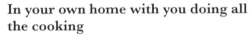

Tips for running a func

by Pam Gregory

The two objectives of a successful dinner are to raise as much money and awareness as possible for your chosen project, and possibly even more importantly, to make sure that everyone has such a wonderful time that they can't wait for the next one! Dinners can be run in a number of ways:

In your own home with you doing all the cooking
You can use the recipes found in this book! This is hard work, but very rewarding. Atmosphere very informal, BYOB, food buffet-style but as sumptuous and varied as possible. Dishes are labelled and if you are supporting a project involving refugees, name the refugee who donated the recipe. Ensure you have an up-to-date presentation about your cause to show while everyone is having a drink before dinner. Charge low ticket prices – I normally charge £10 a head but imply that donations are gratefully accepted. If people love the food, atmosphere and have watched the presentation, they will be generous. Don't worry if you haven't got seating for absolutely everyone. People will wander around with plates of food and stop to chat. Try and do a lighthearted quiz based on the presentation you gave and give a prize to the winner (I usually provide a home-made cake in 'glamorous' wrapping). Be on hand to try and answer any questions your guests might have but don't be afraid to say you don't have all the answers.

With a little help from your friends!
If you're cooking phobic, you could still do all of the above, or you could ring the changes and have a Curry Night, Italian Feast, or Pot Luck

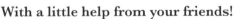

aising dinner

Dinner to which everyone is asked to bring a dish. Because people tend to make what they're best at, you usually end up with a wonderful banquet for which you've cooked only one or two things. Still do the presentation, quiz or similar profile-raising activity. Circulate and chat about the project you are supporting as much as possible. Hint that there will be another dinner soon and they should book early to avoid disappointment!

Get out of the house!
In good weather, organise a BBQ with everyone bringing contributions. Or rent out a large room in your local pub, village hall, barn or community centre to throw a big party run on similar lines to above, where everyone brings a dish to share. Dinners in bigger venues like these go particularly well just before Christmas and can easily be combined with a Promise Auction, where local people donate their services or expertise free of charge. Diners can then bid on each lot, with the money going to your chosen cause. In our village, a tree surgeon donated half a day's work, I donated one glamorous homemade cake every month, and a local yachtsman offered a loch trip on his boat. Babysitting, gardening, guitar lessons – an endless list. There will be so much talent available and you will be astonished at how much an auction can raise. Everyone will go home feeling they've made a positive contribution and also had a really great time.

Don't be scared, rope your friends in and give it a go. Once you've done one, the next one's a walk in the park!

Acknowledgments

We are heavily indebted to Lindsay Maitland-Hunt for the time and knowledge she dedicated to this project. The quality of this book would not have been the same without her valuable input.

Thank you to Margaret Oke for additional editing and cooking, Joel Pearce for edits, cooking and advice and to Shivani Hassard for help getting the project over the finish line with additional photography and support. Thanks too to Donie Brady and Dan Chapman for their help and contributions to the section about Samos Volunteers.

We wanted these recipes to be incredibly tasty and easy to follow and that required a lot of testing! Thank you to our recipe testers: Frances Bevan, Lily Callaway, Kiki Crean, Sue Creech, Lucy Gladstone, Bea Goudy, Abi Gregory, Ellie Gregory, Angela Karacaoglu, Caitlin McLaughlin, Topi Morris, Ella Raeburn, Lorna Selfe, Rose Tolovae and Fiona Wyllie.

Thank you to Joy Jorgensen for loaning a camera, Lauynas and Milda at Kopa books for their patient advice, Ross Ireland for his support and Joyce Yeap for her ongoing help to the project.